Printed in the USA

Esperanto Language:

101 Esperanto Verbs

BY MERITA ALEXANDER

Contents

Introduction to Esperanto verb conjugation

The conjugation of verbs is, by design, much simpler and easier in Esperanto than in English and most other national languages. There are no irregular verbs. A verb's root never changes: we only vary the ending. And unlike in many national languages, the endings never depend on the subject's person, number, gender, etc. All verbs in Esperanto are regular, even **"esti"** (to be).

To see this difference clearly, compare a few example forms of the Esperanto verb "esti" (to be) with corresponding forms in English, German, Spanish, and Polish:

		Esperanto "esti"	English "to be"	German "sein"	Spanish "ser"	Polish "być"
Present		Mi **estas**.	I **am**.	Ich **bin**.	Yo **soy**.	Ja **jestem**.
		Li/ŝi **estas**.	He/she **is**.	Er/sie **ist**.	Él/ella **es**.	On/ona **jest**.
		Ni **estas**.	We **are**.	Wir **sind**.	Nosotros (♂)/ nosotras (♀) **somos**.	My **jesteśmy**.
Past		Mi **estis**.	I **was**.	Ich **war**.	Yo **era**.	Ja **byłem**. (♂) Ja **byłam**. (♀)
		Li/ŝi **estis**.	He/she **was**.	Er/sie **war**.	Él/ella **era**.	On **był**. (♂) Ona **była**. (♀)
		Ni **estis**.	We **were**.	Wir **waren**.	Nosotros (♂)/ nosotras (♀) **éramos**.	My **byliśmy**. (♂) My **byłyśmy**. (♀)
Future		Mi **estos**.	I **will be**.	Ich **werde sein**.	Yo **seré**.	Ja **będę**.
		Li/ŝi **estos**.	He/she **will be**.	Er/sie **wird sein**.	Él/ella **será**.	On/ona **będzie**.
		Ni **estos**.	We **will be**.	Wir **werden sein**.	Nosotros (♂)/ nosotras (♀) **seremos**.	My **będziemy**.

Note the many irregularities in these example Germanic, Romance, and Slavic languages. In these national languages, there is no obvious relation between the various forms of a verb. That is, knowing the English present tense "He **is**" does not help you to know that the past tense is "He **was**", or that the first person present form is "I **am**". You must memorize the various forms of many irregular verbs in English, German, and other national languages, because they are arbitrary, instead of following a simple consistent set of rules.

Esperanto, in contrast, has simple regular conjugation. As the example illustrates, there is a verb with the root **est-**, and endings **-i** for infinitive, **-as** for present, **-is** for past, **-os** for future, all independent of the subject's person, number, or gender. Let us look at the Esperanto verb system in more detail now.

The 6 verb endings:

There are only 6 verb endings in Esperanto. They are applied to the same unchanging root of the verb. E.g. the root "**skrib-**" means "write":

-i = infinitive. **Skribi** = to write.
-as = present indicative. **Mi skribas** = I write, I am writing.
-is = past indicative. **Mi skribis** = I wrote, I was writing, I have written.
-os = future indicative. **Mi skribos** = I will write, I will be writing.
-u = imperative / volitive. **Skribu!** = Write! **Mi skribu!** = I should write! I must write!
-us = conditional. **Mi skribus** = I would write, I would be writing, I would have written.

If a word does not have one of those 6 endings, then it is not a verb! Notice also that no syntactical distinction is made among various grammatical aspects of the verb, unlike these obligatory distinctions in English. The context generally makes these distinctions clear, so there is no need in Esperanto for an obligatory syntactical distinction. Here are some examples:

Grammatical aspect	English	Esperanto
Present simple	I **write** books.	Mi **skribas** librojn.
Present progressive	I **am writing** a book now.	Mi **skribas** libron nun.
Present perfect	I **have written** three books.	Mi **skribis** tri librojn.
Past simple	I **wrote** a book yesterday.	Mi **skribis** libron hieraŭ.
Past progressive	While I **was writing**, he visited.	Dum mi **skribis**, li vizitis.
Simple future	I **will write** a book someday.	Mi **skribos** libron iam.
Future progressive	While I **will be writing**, he will visit.	Dum mi **skribos**, li vizitos.
Future perfect	I **will have written** the book before you visit.	Mi **skribos** la libron antaŭ ol vi vizitos.

Notice how English requires quite varied syntax for the verb form, depending on the tense and whether the action was completed or continuous, often with auxiliary / helping verbs (some form of "to be" or "to have") or other extra words (e.g. "will"). In Esperanto, none of that exists. We simply use the verb ending **-as** for present actions, **-is** for past actions, and **-os** for future actions. The context typically makes the nuances of verbal aspect clear. Also, certain other words give helpful information about the specific nuance of a verb: for example, a sentence starting with "**dum**" ("while") generally indicates a progressive / continuous / ongoing action.

2

Tip: A common error for many English speakers learning another language is to mistakenly translate each *word* in the English sentence literally, in isolation, instead of translating the *meaning* of the entire *sentence*. They mistakenly translate English sentences like "I am writing" and "I have written a book" into invalid Esperanto like *Mi estas skribas* and *Mi havas skribis libron*. It is important to understand that in those English sentences, the words "am" and "have" are merely *mandatory elements of syntax* for the verb tenses in the sentences - the *meanings* of the sentences "I am writing" and "I have written a book" have *nothing* to do with the English verbs "to be" and "to have"! The real *verb* in both sentences is "to write" (in the present progressive and the present perfect, respectively): the sentences are about *writing*, not about *being* or *having*. So the auxiliary "to be" and "to have", which are just formal syntax required by English, should *not* be translated individually as words into another language. They are simply syntax which signals that the sentences are talking about actions in the present (therefore "Mi skrib**as**" in Esperanto) and in the past (therefore "Mi skrib**is** libron" in Esperanto).

Pronunciation

The rules of Esperanto pronunciation are simple and completely regular (unlike in English), and they apply to verbs just like to all other words in Esperanto: each letter is sounded independently in sequence, each letter has a single sound independent of context, each of the 5 vowels (a, e, i, o, u) creates an individual syllable (remember that "ŭ" is not a vowel, but similar to English "w"), and in any multisyllable word, the accent always falls on the next-to-last syllable. So the verb "legas" (reads) has 2 syllables, with the accent on the first syllable ("*le*-gas"). The verb "forgesis" (forgot) has 3 syllables, with the accent on the middle syllable ("for-*ge*-sis"). The verb "asocii" (to associate) has 4 syllables, with the accent on the third syllable ("a-so-*ci*-i").

Mi *skri*bis *lib*ron hi*e*raŭ. (I wrote a book yesterday.)
Mi *pa*gos vin *ki*am vi vi*zi*tos ho*di*aŭ. (I will pay you when you visit today.)
*Ki*al vi *le*gas *lib*ron? (Why are you reading a book?)
Ĉu *i*li *ve*nos? (Will they come?)
Li ne*ni*am *trin*kas bi*e*ron. (He never drinks beer.)

Negative sentences

Negating a sentence is simpler and more regular in Esperanto than in English. We usually simply use "**ne**" before the verb.
I write books. I **do not write** books. = Mi skribas librojn. Mi **ne skribas** librojn.
He was writing. He **was not writing**. = Li skribis. Li **ne skribis**.
She wrote a book. She **did not write** a book. = Ŝi skribis libron. Ŝi **ne skribis** libron.

Esperanto does not use "double negatives", unlike some languages, e.g. Spanish and Polish. So in sentences with "**neniam**" (never), "**neniu**" (nobody), etc, we do *not* use "ne" for emphasis. So:

I never drink wine. = Mi neniam trinkas vinon. (*Not* *Mi neniam ne trinkas vinon*!)
Nobody saw me. = Neniu vidis min. (*Not* *Neniu ne vidis min*!)
He said nothing. = Li diris nenion. (*Not* *Li ne diris nenion*!)
A sentence like "Mi neniam ne trinkas vinon" with "neniam" *and* "ne" is interpreted logically to mean "I **never** do **not** drink wine", i.e. "I **always** drink wine, there is **no** time when I am **not** drinking wine."

Questions

Questions do not cause the verb to have different word order or very different syntax in Esperanto, unlike in English.
To form a yes-no question, we can simply add the question word "**ĉu**" to the start of a sentence, leaving the rest of the sentence unchanged:

He is writing. Is he writing? = Li skribas. **Ĉu** li skribas?
We wrote. Did we write? = Ni skribis. **Ĉu** ni skribis?
You are reading a book. Are you reading a book? = Vi legas libron. **Ĉu** vi legas libron?
They will come. Will they come? = Ili venos. **Ĉu** ili venos?

Additionally the various correlatives beginning with "**ki-**" can be used to introduce a question.
Why are you reading a book? = **Kial** vi legas libron?
Where are you reading a book? = **Kie** vi legas libron?
When are you reading a book? = **Kiam** vi legas libron?
How are you reading a book? = **Kiel** vi legas libron?
With whom are you reading a book? = **Kun kiu** vi legas libron?
Which book are you reading? = **Kiun** libron vi legas?
What are you reading? = **Kion** vi legas?

Verb subjects and direct objects

Generally subjects and direct objects in Esperanto work similarly to English. The subject is always in the nominative case (singular **-o**, plural **-oj** for ordinary nouns), and direct objects are always in the accusative case (singular **-on**, plural **-ojn** for ordinary nouns; **-n** for pronouns). In English, these cases are explicitly distinguished by different forms of a word only with pronouns ("I see him", not *Me see he*), not with ordinary nouns. In Esperanto, as in many languages, the accusative ending is applied to all direct objects. Examples:

The people are buying **tickets**. = La homoj aĉetas **biletojn**.
The people bought **tickets**. = La homoj aĉetis **biletojn**.
She bought a **ticket**. = Ŝi aĉetis **bileton**.
I will buy a **ticket**. = Mi aĉetos **bileton**.
I see **him**. = Mi vidas **lin**.
He sees **me**. = Li vidas **min**.

Typically, the word order in a sentence is the same as in English: subject-verb-object. But because word order is flexible in Esperanto, all 6 possible orders of subject, verb, object are valid:

La viro trinkis akvon. (usual S-V-O)	La viro akvon trinkis. (S-O-V)
Akvon trinkis la viro. (O-V-S)	Akvon la viro trinkis. (O-S-V)
Trinkis la viro akvon. (V-S-O)	Trinkis akvon la viro. (V-O-S)

One might use a less common word order for particular emphasis, nuance, poetic rhythm, personal taste, or other stylistic reason. (E.g. "Ne *bieron*, sed *akvon* li trinkis!" = He didn't drink *beer*, but *water*!) This is flexible, and there are no absolute rules concerning this.

Participles

There exist present, past, and future adjectival participle endings in Esperanto. Formally these are not verb tenses, but simply adjectives (and thus they take the 4 usual adjectival endings: **-a, -aj, -an, -ajn** for singular nominative, plural nominative, singular accusative, plural accusative). They can be used simply as adjectives, and also to express nuance in sentences similar to English sentences with participle verb forms.

-ant- = present active participle
-int- = past active participle
-ont- = future active participle
-at- = present passive participle
-it- = past passive participle
-ot- = future passive participle

Notice that the same vowels (**a, i, o**) appear in the present, past, future forms here as in the corresponding verb endings (**-as, -is, -os**). The active and passive forms are similar to each other: the only difference is the presence or absence of **n** in the middle.

Because the participles in Esperanto are grammatically adjectives, they can be used anywhere an adjective can be used, and they take the appropriate ending for case and number just like any other adjective. So they can simply appear directly with a noun, as an attribute:

The beautiful **smiling** woman watched the **sleeping** old man. = La bela **ridetanta** virino rigardis la **dormantan** maljunan viron.
The **laughing** boys chased the **running** cats. = La **ridantaj** knaboj ĉasis la **kurantajn** katojn.
The **lost** book disappeared yesterday. = La **perdita** libro malaperis hieraŭ.
We found the **lost** valuable book. = Ni trovis la **perditan** valoran libron.

They can also be used predicatively (with the verb "esti", to be) to describe a subject, but often we simply use a basic verb form for this kind of sentence:
She **is dancing**. = Ŝi **estas dancanta**. (emphasizes the ongoing action) = Ŝi **dancas**. (more usual form)
The people **are dancing**. = La homoj **estas dancantaj**. (plural noun & adjective endings) = La homoj **dancas**.
We **are drinking** water. = Ni **estas trinkantaj** akvon. = Ni **trinkas** akvon.

The beautiful dancing people **were laughing**. = La belaj dancantaj homoj **estis ridantaj** = La belaj dancantaj homoj **ridis**.

Note that in the English sentence "She is dancing", we would consider the *verb* to be a present progressive form of "to dance", but in the rather literally translated equivalent Esperanto sentence "Ŝi estas dancanta", the *verb* is "estas" (with the present tense verb ending **-as**), while "dancantaj" is simply an ***adjective*** (which happens to be a participle), the same way that in the sentence "Ŝi estas bela" (She is beautiful), the verb is "estas" and "bela" is an adjective (which happens not to be a participle). In the less literally translated and more typical Esperanto sentence "Ŝi dancas", the *verb* is "dancas".

Since adjectives can themselves function as verbs simply by adding a verb ending, a participle is no exception:
She **is dancing.** = Ŝi **dancas.** = Ŝi **estas dancanta.** = Ŝi **dancantas**.
But a participle used as a verb, such as "dancantas", is generally quite redundant and very rarely used.

The affix **-ad-** can be used to explicitly express continual activity:
Ŝi danc**ad**as.
That is a more natural and typical form than "Ŝi danc**ant**as".

Action on the subject (passive forms)

A transitive verb is used to show that a subject performs some action on an object. For example:
I am reading a book. = Mi legas libron. (Book/libron is the direct object.)
She drank wine. = Ŝi trinkis vinon. (Wine/vinon is the direct object.)

Active forms are more commonly used in Esperanto than passive forms, just like in English and many other languages. But passive forms are sometimes useful, or desirable for stylistic reasons. There are 2 common ways to achieve a passive effect (action on the subject) with a transitive verb in Esperanto:

1. Passive participle.
A passive participle can be used as an adjective to show that a noun receives an action, just as we use an active participle to show that a noun performs an action. In practice, we can often use "de" or "fare de" to identify the agent in this sort of passive sentence:

I was reading a book. = Mi legis libron. (active)
The book was **read** by me. = La libro estis **legita** de mi. (passive)
I found the **lost** book. = Mi trovis la **perditan** libron. (active sentence with passive adjective describing object)
The **lost** book was **found** by me. = La **perdita** libro estis **trovita** de mi. (passive sentence with passive adjective describing the subject)
The book was **written** by my friend. = La libro estis **skribita** fare de mia amiko.

2. The affix **-iĝ-**.
We can insert **-iĝ-** before a transitive verb's ending to cause its action to be applied to the *subject* instead of to a direct object. This type of sentence less commonly includes identification of the agent.

I lost the book. = Mi perdis la libron. (active)
The book **was lost**. = La libro **perdiĝis**. (passive)
I read the book and returned it to the library. = Mi legis la libron kaj redonis ĝin al la biblioteko. (active)
The book was **read** and **returned**. = La libro **legiĝis** kaj **redoniĝis**. (passive)
The guard saw me. = La gardisto vidis min. (active)
I **was seen**. = Mi **vidiĝis**. (passive)

State changes

The affix **-iĝ-** is used also to show a transition into a new state. For example it can be used with an adjective, either forming a single verb (root + **iĝ** + verb ending) or using **iĝ-** (or **fariĝ-**, from the root "fari", to make or do) as its own verb with a separate adjective:

He **became red** due to shame. = Li **ruĝiĝis** pro honto. = Li iĝis ruĝa pro honto.
Her face **became pale** due to shock. = Ŝia vizaĝo **paliĝis** pro ŝoko. = Ŝia vizaĝo fariĝis pala pro ŝoko.
The running cat **will become tired**. = La kuranta kato **laciĝos**. = La kuranta kato iĝos laca.

The affix **-iĝ-** can also be used with intransitive verbs to indicate a change of state. For example the verbs "sidi" (to sit) and "stari" (to stand) are intransitive (they do not take direct objects) but simply show what state the subject is in.

He was sitting. = Li sidis. (He was continually sitting, with no change in his state.)
He **sat down**. = Li **sidiĝis**. (He changed from a standing to a seated position.)
He is standing. = Li staras. (He is continually standing, with no change in his state.)
He **is standing up**. = Li **stariĝas**. (He is changing from a seated to a standing position.)

This can also be done with the prefix **ek-** (which often has a nuance of a more sudden state change).

He sat down. = Li sidiĝis. = Li **ek**sidis.
He is standing up. = Li stariĝas. = Li **ek**staras.

Imperative

The imperative (**-u**) verb ending is often used in non-indicative sentences which are direct commands, statements of obligation, and proposals:
Read the book! = **Legu** la libron!
We **should read** the book. = Ni **legu** la libron.

Let's read the book. = Ni **legu** la libron.

Questions can also be formed from such imperative sentences, simply by adding **ĉu** (for yes-no questions) or one of the correlatives to the start of the sentence:
Should we read the book? = **Ĉu** ni legu la libron?
When should we read the book? = **Kiam** ni legu la libron?
Where should we read the book? = **Kie** ni legu la libron?

It is also used to express someone's will in a subordinate clause in sentences and questions like the following, which use "**ke**" (that) and the imperative:
They want me **to read** the book. = Ili volas, ke mi **legu** la libron.
They ordered me **not to read** the book. = Ili ordonis, ke mi **ne legu** la libron.
Do you want me **to give** you the book? = **Ĉu** vi volas, ke mi **donu** la libron al vi?
When do they want me **to read** the book? = **Kiam** ili volas, ke mi **legu** la libron?

A very common idiom is to use the imperative form "Bonvolu" plus an infinitive for polite requests, where we would often use "Please" in English. (Grammatically you are literally being requested to "kindly/willingly" do something which is then expressed with the infinitive.)

Please give me the book. = **Bonvolu doni** la libron al mi.
Please stand there. = **Bonvolu stari** tie.
Please come with me. = **Bonvolu veni** kun mi.

A variant form uses the adverb form "bonvole" before or after the imperative of the other (requested) verb. (Grammatically the adverb "bonvole" literally tells how you should perform the verb: "kindly/willingly".)

Bonvolu **doni** la libron al mi. = **Donu** bonvole la libron al mi.
Bonvolu **stari** tie. = **Staru** bonvole tie.
Bonvolu **veni** kun mi. = **Venu** bonvole kun mi.
But do not use the **u**-ending twice in these forms. *Bonvolu donu la libron* is invalid. Use either "Bonvolu doni" or "Bonvole donu" = "Donu bonvole".

Conditional

The conditional (-**us**) verb ending is used for conditional and counter-factual sentences, which typically use the word "**se**" (if) to introduce the conditional part.

If I **were** rich, I **would live** in Paris. = Se mi **estus** riĉa, mi **loĝus** en Parizo. (In reality, I'm not rich and I don't live in Paris.)
If you **would help** me, I **would finish** the task quickly. = Se vi **helpus** min, mi **finus** la taskon rapide. (In reality, you are not helping me, so I won't finish the task quickly.)

As in many languages, this form can also be used to express politeness in a request or order:
I would like you to finish the task. = Mi **volus**, ke vi finu la taskon.

I would like some help. = Mi **dezirus** helpon.
Would you give me the book? = Ĉu vi **donus** al mi la libron?
Would you be so good as to help me? = Ĉu vi **bonvolus** helpi min?

Note that the conditional -us does not indicate past, present or future. The context typically makes it clear. In case of doubt, it is possible to use a past, present or future participle to make the tense explicitly clear.

When I was in Germany, I **would have visited** Berlin but I didn't have time.
= Kiam mi estis en Germanujo, mi **vizitus** Berlinon, sed mi ne havis tempon.
= Kiam mi estis en Germanujo, mi **estus vizitinta** Berlinon, sed mi ne havis tempon.
= Kiam mi estis en Germanujo, mi **vizitintus** Berlinon, sed mi ne havis tempon.

We would visit Berlin during our next trip, but it won't be possible.
= Ni **vizitus** Berlinon dum nia sekva vojaĝo, sed ne eblos.
= Ni **estus vizitontaj** Berlinon dum nia sekva vojaĝo, sed ne eblos.
= Ni **vizitontus** Berlinon dum nia sekva vojaĝo, sed ne eblos.

Infinitive

The infintive (**-i**) verb ending is used in many of the same ways as the English infinitive, to name an action or state.

I want **to eat**. = Mi volas **manĝi**.
She likes **to read** science fiction. = Ŝi ŝatas **legi** sciencfikcion.
They needed **to finish** the task. = Ili bezonis **fini** la taskon.
We should **leave**. = Ni devas **foriri**.
I would like **to sleep**. = Mi ŝatus **dormi**.
Can I **sit** there? = Ĉu mi povas **sidi** tie?
May we **come** tomorrow? = Ĉu ni rajtas **veni** morgaŭ?
Will you help me **finish** the task? = Ĉu vi helpos min **fini** la taskon?
He started **to work**. = Li komencis **labori**.
They asked me **to leave**. = Ili petis min **foriri**.

Note that there is no auxiliary word like "to", which is usually needed in English in such sentences (but not always in English, e.g. with "should", "must", "may", "can").

An infinitive can also be used like a noun subject, but it is still a verb, so it is described by an adverb, not an adjective as in English. We often use the **-ing** form of a verb in English to express this kind of sentence, but in Esperanto, the infinitive (**-i**) is used.

Staying with a lion is **dangerous**. = **Resti** kun leono estas **danĝere**. (*Not* *danĝera*!
"Resti" is a verb, so we modify it with an adverb, not an adjective.)
Playing chess was **popular** in Poland. = **Ludi** ŝakon estis **populare** en Polujo.
Reading books educates us. = **Legi** librojn edukas nin.

Reading every day helps us **learn**. = **Legi** ĉiutage helpas nin **lerni**.

An infinitive, as in English, can express purpose. Often we use "**por**" (for) with it for clarity.

I came **to see** you. = Mi venis **por vidi** vin. = Mi venis **vidi** vin.
He will buy a book **to give** her. = Li aĉetos libron **por doni** al ŝi.
The dog is running **to catch** the cat. = La hundo kuras **por kapti** la katon.
Did she come to listen to the music? = Ĉu ŝi venis **por aŭskulti** la muzikon?

The use of -ig-

The affix "**-ig-**" can be used to cause a direct object to perform the root verb, instead of the subject performing it. It is often useful for situations where English might say "I caused ...", "I made ...".

I was reading. = Mi **legis**. (The subject "I" was reading.)
I made the child read. = Mi **legigis** la infanon. (The direct object "child" was reading.)
He will eat. = Li **manĝos**. (The subject "He" will eat.)
He will feed the dog. = Li **manĝigos** la hundon. (The direct object "dog" will eat.)
The teacher is speaking. = La instruisto **parolas**.
The teacher is making the learners speak. = La instruisto **paroligas** la lernantojn.

Perhaps surprisingly, -ig- can *also* be used to cause the root verb to be performed upon the direct object (by someone other than the subject). This may seem confusing or ambiguous, but the context usually makes it obvious which way -ig- is being used.

The workers constructed a pyramid. = La laboristoj **konstruis** piramidon.
The pharaoh caused a pyramid to be built. = La faraono **konstruigis** piramidon. (The pyramid was constructed.)
The pharaoh made the workers build. = La faraono **konstruigis** la laboristojn. (The workers were forced to work.)

Verb transitivity

English is very loose about verb transitivity: many verbs have two separate meanings (intransitively acting on the subject, or transitively acting on the direct object.) For example, in English "to commence" and "to begin" and "to start" can all mean that the *subject* is commencing ("The concert commenced/started/began"), or that the subject is commencing the direct object ("The band commenced/started/began the concert"). The Esperanto verb "komenci" has strictly the second transitive usage, with the verb's subject acting upon a direct object: "La bando **komencis** la koncerton". It is a common error to say *La koncerto komencis.*

English speakers learning another language often make errors when they simply memorize lists of foreign verbs with "English equivalents". It is important to learn the *meanings* of verbs in another language (e.g. "komenci" means "to cause something to begin", so it needs a direct object), instead of simply memorizing "English equivalents" (e.g. if one simply remembers that "komenci = to begin, to start", one will make mistakes using "komenci" in Esperanto, since the English "equivalent" has additional meaning not present in "komenci".) Similarly for "to finish" and "to end" and "to stop": these English verbs have 2 different meanings ("The concert finished" vs "The band finished the concert"), but in Esperanto, the verb "fini" means that the subject causes the direct object to finish, not that the subject itself finishes. For verbs like "komenci" and "fini", if you want the subject itself to be starting or ending, you need to use the -**iĝ**- affix:

The student started the task. = La studento **komencis** la taskon.
The concert started. = La koncerto **komenciĝis**. (*Not:* *La koncerto komencis*! This is a common error!)
I will finish the task tomorrow. = Mi **finos** la taskon morgaŭ.
The concert will finish soon. = La koncerto **finiĝos** baldaŭ. (*Not:* *La koncerto finos baldaŭ*!)

Conversely, there are Esperanto verbs which affect the subject and can't have a direct object (just like the English verb "to die", for example: "He is dying", but not *He is dying the cat*; in English, we'd have to use a different verb, e.g. "He is killing the cat."). The verb "droni" means "to die in water", so it cannot have a direct object, unlike the English verb "to drown". The verb "kreski" means "to become larger", so it cannot have a direct object, unlike the English verb "to grow".

The child drowned in the river. = La infano **dronis** en la rivero.
The man drowned the cat in the river. = La viro dron**ig**is la katon en la rivero. (*Not:* *La viro dronis la katon en la rivero*! This is a common error!)
The plant will grow. = La planto **kreskos**.
The gardener is growing plants. = La ĝardenisto **kreskigas** plantojn. (*Not:* *La ĝardenisto kreskas plantojn*!)

Subjectless verbs

English often uses "it" as a meaningless but syntactically necessary grammatical subject, e.g. "It is raining." In that sentence, "it" does not really refer to anything. In Esperanto verbs like "pluvi" (to rain), which don't have a meaningful subject but simply represent some subjectless action, do not need a grammatical subject. A common error is translating such "dummy" it-subjects literally to "ĝi" (it) in Esperanto.

It **is raining**. = **Pluvas**. (*Not:* *Ĝi pluvas*!)

It **will snow** tomorrow. = **Neĝos** morgaŭ. (*Not:* *Ĝi neĝos*!)

It **is possible** that it **will rain**. = **Eblas**, ke **pluvos**. (*Not:* *Ĝi eblas, ke ĝi pluvos*!)

Esperanto verb table

Here is a sample Esperanto verb (*akcepti*) conjugated, fully showing all traditional forms of the indicative (present, past, future; singular, plural; 1st, 2nd, 3rd persons). Note that the form does not depend on number or person:

to accept	infinitive	imperative	conditional
	ak**cep**ti	ak**cep**tu	ak**cep**tus

indicative	present	past	future
I	mi ak**cep**tas	mi ak**cep**tis	mi ak**cep**tos
you *(singular)*	vi ak**cep**tas	vi ak**cep**tis	vi ak**cep**tos
he/she/it	li/ŝi/ĝi ak**cep**tas	li/ŝi/ĝi ak**cep**tis	li/ŝi/ĝi ak**cep**tos
we	ni ak**cep**tas	ni ak**cep**tis	ni ak**cep**tos
you *(plural)*	vi ak**cep**tas	vi ak**cep**tis	vi ak**cep**tos
they	ili ak**cep**tas	ili ak**cep**tis	ili ak**cep**tos

	present	past	future
active participles	akcept**an**ta	akcept**in**ta	akcept**on**ta
passive participles	akcept**a**ta	akcept**i**ta	akcept**o**ta

Because the indicative form depends *only* on the verb tense (present, past, or future), in the series of 101 verb tables which follow only the 3 indicative forms (present, past, and future) are shown, and not all 6 combinations of person and number for each tense.

The participle forms are shown, even though formally participles are adjectives in Esperanto (and take adjective endings), since participles are nonetheless closely related to verbs. Note that a few verbs have no passive participles, because those verbs are completely intransitive and never have a direct object, for example *esti* (to be) and *iĝi* (to become).

A word's accent always falls on the next to last syllable in Esperanto.

13

to accept	infinitive	imperative	conditional
	ak**cep**ti	ak**cep**tu	ak**cep**tus

indicative	present	past	future
	ak**cep**tas	ak**cep**tis	ak**cep**tos

	present	past	future
active participles	akcep**tan**ta	akcep**tin**ta	akcep**ton**ta
passive participles	akcep**tat**a	akcep**tit**a	akcep**tot**a

to admit, confess	infinitive	imperative	conditional
	kon**fes**i	kon**fes**u	kon**fes**us

indicative	present	past	future
	kon**fes**as	kon**fes**is	kon**fes**os

	present	past	future
active participles	konfe**san**ta	konfe**sin**ta	konfe**son**ta
passive participles	konfe**sat**a	konfe**sit**a	konfe**sot**a

to answer	infinitive	imperative	conditional
	res**pon**di	res**pon**du	res**pon**dus

indicative	present	past	future
	res**pon**das	res**pon**dis	res**pon**dos

	present	past	future
active participles	respon**dan**ta	respon**din**ta	respon**don**ta
passive participles	respon**dat**a	respon**dit**a	respon**dot**a

to appear, become visible, come into sight	infinitive	imperative	conditional
	aperi	**ap**eru	**ap**erus

indicative	present	past	future
	aperas	**ap**eris	**ap**eros

	present	past	future
active participles	ape**ran**ta	ape**rin**ta	ape**ron**ta

to ask, seek information	infinitive	imperative	conditional
	de**man**di	de**man**du	de**man**dus

indicative	present	past	future
	de**man**das	de**man**dis	de**man**dos

	present	past	future
active participles	deman**dan**ta	deman**din**ta	deman**don**ta
passive participles	deman**dat**a	deman**dit**a	deman**dot**a

to be	infinitive	imperative	conditional
	esti	**es**tu	**es**tus

indicative	present	past	future
	estas	**es**tis	**es**tos

	present	past	future
active participles	est**an**ta	est**in**ta	est**on**ta

to be able to	infinitive	imperative	conditional
	povi	**po**vu	**po**vus

indicative	present	past	future
	povas	**po**vis	**po**vos

	present	past	future
active participles	po**van**ta	po**vin**ta	po**von**ta
passive participles	po**va**ta	po**vi**ta	po**vo**ta

to become, turn into	infinitive	imperative	conditional
	iĝi	**i**ĝu	**i**ĝus

indicative	present	past	future
	iĝas	**i**ĝis	**i**ĝos

	present	past	future
active participles	i**ĝan**ta	i**ĝin**ta	i**ĝon**ta

to begin something	infinitive	imperative	conditional
	ko**men**ci	ko**men**cu	ko**men**cus

indicative	present	past	future
	ko**men**cas	ko**men**cis	ko**men**cos

	present	past	future
active participles	komen**can**ta	komen**cin**ta	komen**con**ta
passive participles	komen**ca**ta	komen**ci**ta	komen**co**ta

to break	infinitive	imperative	conditional
	rompi	**rom**pu	**rom**pus

indicative	present	past	future
	rompas	**rom**pis	**rom**pos

	present	past	future
active participles	rom**pan**ta	rom**pin**ta	rom**pon**ta
passive participles	rom**pa**ta	rom**pi**ta	rom**po**ta

to breathe	infinitive	imperative	conditional
	spiri	**spi**ru	**spi**rus

indicative	present	past	future
	spiras	**spi**ris	**spi**ros

	present	past	future
active participles	spi**ran**ta	spi**rin**ta	spi**ron**ta
passive participles	spi**ra**ta	spi**ri**ta	spi**ro**ta

to buy, purchase	infinitive	imperative	conditional
	a**ĉe**ti	a**ĉe**tu	a**ĉe**tus

indicative	present	past	future
	a**ĉe**tas	a**ĉe**tis	a**ĉe**tos

	present	past	future
active participles	aĉe**tan**ta	aĉe**tin**ta	aĉe**ton**ta
passive participles	aĉe**ta**ta	aĉe**ti**ta	aĉe**to**ta

to call	infinitive	imperative	conditional
	voki	**vo**ku	**vo**kus

indicative	present	past	future
	vokas	**vo**kis	**vo**kos

	present	past	future
active participles	vo**kan**ta	vo**kin**ta	vo**kon**ta
passive participles	vo**ka**ta	vo**ki**ta	vo**ko**ta

to can, be able to	infinitive	imperative	conditional
	povi	**po**vu	**po**vus

indicative	present	past	future
	povas	**po**vis	**po**vos

	present	past	future
active participles	po**van**ta	po**vin**ta	po**von**ta
passive participles	po**va**ta	po**vi**ta	po**vo**ta

to choose	infinitive	imperative	conditional
	e**lek**ti	e**lek**tu	e**lek**tus

indicative	present	past	future
	e**lek**tas	e**lek**tis	e**lek**tos

	present	past	future
active participles	elek**tan**ta	elek**tin**ta	elek**ton**ta
passive participles	elek**ta**ta	elek**ti**ta	elek**to**ta

to close something	infinitive	imperative	conditional
	fermi	**fer**mu	**fer**mus

indicative	present	past	future
	fermas	**fer**mis	**fer**mos

	present	past	future
active participles	fer**man**ta	fer**min**ta	fer**mon**ta
passive participles	fer**ma**ta	fer**mi**ta	fer**mo**ta

to come	infinitive	imperative	conditional
	veni	**v**enu	**v**enus

indicative	present	past	future
	venas	**v**enis	**v**enos

	present	past	future
active participles	ven**an**ta	ven**in**ta	ven**on**ta

to cook	infinitive	imperative	conditional
	kuiri	kuiru	kuirus

indicative	present	past	future
	kuiras	kuiris	kuiros

	present	past	future
active participles	kuir**an**ta	kuir**in**ta	kuir**on**ta
passive participles	kuir**a**ta	kuir**i**ta	kuir**o**ta

to cry, to weep	infinitive	imperative	conditional
	plori	**plo**ru	**plo**rus

indicative	present	past	future
	ploras	**plo**ris	**plo**ros

	present	past	future
active participles	plo**ran**ta	plo**rin**ta	plo**ron**ta
passive participles	plo**ra**ta	plo**ri**ta	plo**ro**ta

to dance	infinitive	imperative	conditional
	danci	**dan**cu	**dan**cus

indicative	present	past	future
	dancas	**dan**cis	**dan**cos

	present	past	future
active participles	dan**can**ta	dan**cin**ta	dan**con**ta
passive participles	dan**ca**ta	dan**ci**ta	dan**co**ta

to decide	infinitive	imperative	conditional
	de**ci**di	de**ci**du	de**ci**dus

indicative	present	past	future
	de**ci**das	de**ci**dis	de**ci**dos

	present	past	future
active participles	deci**dan**ta	deci**din**ta	deci**don**ta
passive participles	deci**da**ta	deci**di**ta	deci**do**ta

to decrease, make something smaller	infinitive	imperative	conditional
	malpliigi	malpliigu	malpliigus

indicative	present	past	future
	malpliigas	malpliigis	malpliigos

	present	past	future
active participles	malpliiganta	malpliiginta	malpliigonta
passive participles	malpliigata	malpliigita	malpliigota

to die	infinitive	imperative	conditional
	morti	mortu	mortus

indicative	present	past	future
	mortas	mortis	mortos

	present	past	future
active participles	mortanta	mortinta	mortonta

to do	infinitive	imperative	conditional
	fari	faru	farus

indicative	present	past	future
	faras	faris	faros

	present	past	future
active participles	faranta	farinta	faronta
passive participles	farata	farita	farota

to drink	infinitive	imperative	conditional
	trinki	**trin**ku	**trin**kus

indicative	present	past	future
	trinkas	**trin**kis	**trin**kos

	present	past	future
active participles	trink**an**ta	trink**in**ta	trink**on**ta
passive participles	trink**a**ta	trink**i**ta	trink**o**ta

to drive	infinitive	imperative	conditional
	stiri	**sti**ru	**sti**rus

indicative	present	past	future
	stiras	**sti**ris	**sti**ros

	present	past	future
active participles	stir**an**ta	stir**in**ta	stir**on**ta
passive participles	stir**a**ta	stir**i**ta	stir**o**ta

to eat	infinitive	imperative	conditional
	manĝi	**man**ĝu	**man**ĝus

indicative	present	past	future
	manĝas	**man**ĝis	**man**ĝos

	present	past	future
active participles	manĝ**an**ta	manĝ**in**ta	manĝ**on**ta
passive participles	manĝ**a**ta	manĝ**i**ta	manĝ**o**ta

to enter, go in	infinitive	imperative	conditional
	eniri	eniru	enirus

indicative	present	past	future
	eniras	eniris	eniros

	present	past	future
active participles	eniranta	enirinta	enironta
passive participles	enirata	enirita	enirota

to exit, go out	infinitive	imperative	conditional
	eliri	eliru	elirus

indicative	present	past	future
	eliras	eliris	eliros

	present	past	future
active participles	eliranta	elirinta	elironta
passive participles	elirata	elirita	elirota

to explain	infinitive	imperative	conditional
	klarigi	klarigu	klarigus

indicative	present	past	future
	klarigas	klarigis	klarigos

	present	past	future
active participles	klariganta	klariginta	klarigonta
passive participles	klarigata	klarigita	klarigota

to fall	infinitive	imperative	conditional
	fali	**fa**lu	**fa**lus

indicative	present	past	future
	falas	**fa**lis	**fa**los

	present	past	future
active participles	fa**lan**ta	fa**lin**ta	fa**lon**ta
passive participles	fa**lat**a	fa**lit**a	fa**lot**a

to feel	infinitive	imperative	conditional
	senti	**sen**tu	**sen**tus

indicative	present	past	future
	sentas	**sen**tis	**sen**tos

	present	past	future
active participles	sent**an**ta	sent**in**ta	sent**on**ta
passive participles	sent**at**a	sent**it**a	sent**ot**a

to fight	infinitive	imperative	conditional
	batali	**bata**lu	**bata**lus

indicative	present	past	future
	batalas	**bata**lis	**bata**los

	present	past	future
active participles	bata**lan**ta	bata**lin**ta	bata**lon**ta
passive participles	bata**lat**a	bata**lit**a	bata**lot**a

to find	infinitive	imperative	conditional
	trovi	**tro**vu	**tro**vus

indicative	present	past	future
	trovas	**tro**vis	**tro**vos

	present	past	future
active participles	trov**an**ta	trov**in**ta	trov**on**ta
passive participles	trov**a**ta	trov**i**ta	trov**o**ta

to finish something	infinitive	imperative	conditional
	fini	**fi**nu	**fi**nus

indicative	present	past	future
	finas	**fi**nis	**fi**nos

	present	past	future
active participles	fin**an**ta	fin**in**ta	fin**on**ta
passive participles	fin**a**ta	fin**i**ta	fin**o**ta

to fly	infinitive	imperative	conditional
	flugi	**flu**gu	**flu**gus

indicative	present	past	future
	flugas	**flu**gis	**flu**gos

	present	past	future
active participles	flug**an**ta	flug**in**ta	flug**on**ta

to forget	infinitive	imperative	conditional
	forgesi	forgesu	forgesus

indicative	present	past	future
	forgesas	forgesis	forgesos

	present	past	future
active participles	forgesanta	forgesinta	forgesonta
passive participles	forgesata	forgesita	forgesota

to get up, stand up	infinitive	imperative	conditional
	ekstari	ekstaru	ekstarus

indicative	present	past	future
	ekstaras	ekstaris	ekstaros

	present	past	future
active participles	ekstaranta	ekstarinta	ekstaronta

to give	infinitive	imperative	conditional
	doni	donu	donus

indicative	present	past	future
	donas	donis	donos

	present	past	future
active participles	donanta	doninta	dononta
passive participles	donata	donita	donota

to go	infinitive	imperative	conditional
	iri	iru	irus

indicative	present	past	future
	iras	iris	iros

	present	past	future
active participles	**ir**an**ta**	**ir**in**ta**	**ir**on**ta**

to happen	infinitive	imperative	conditional
	o**ka**zi	o**ka**zu	o**ka**zus

indicative	present	past	future
	o**ka**zas	o**ka**zis	o**ka**zos

	present	past	future
active participles	oka**zan**ta	oka**zin**ta	oka**zon**ta

to have	infinitive	imperative	conditional
	havi	**ha**vu	**ha**vus

indicative	present	past	future
	havas	**ha**vis	**ha**vos

	present	past	future
active participles	ha**van**ta	ha**vin**ta	ha**von**ta
passive participles	ha**va**ta	ha**vi**ta	ha**vo**ta

to hear	infinitive	imperative	conditional
	aŭdi	**aŭ**du	**aŭ**dus

indicative	present	past	future
	aŭdas	**aŭ**dis	**aŭ**dos

	present	past	future
active participles	aŭ**dan**ta	aŭ**din**ta	aŭ**don**ta
passive participles	aŭ**da**ta	aŭ**di**ta	aŭ**do**ta

to help	infinitive	imperative	conditional
	helpi	**hel**pu	**hel**pus

indicative	present	past	future
	helpas	**hel**pis	**hel**pos

	present	past	future
active participles	hel**pan**ta	hel**pin**ta	hel**pon**ta
passive participles	hel**pa**ta	hel**pi**ta	hel**po**ta

to hold	infinitive	imperative	conditional
	teni	**te**nu	**te**nus

indicative	present	past	future
	tenas	**te**nis	**te**nos

	present	past	future
active participles	te**nan**ta	te**nin**ta	te**non**ta
passive participles	te**na**ta	te**ni**ta	te**no**ta

to increase, to make larger	infinitive	imperative	conditional
	pliigi	pliigu	pliigus

indicative	present	past	future
	pliigas	pliigis	pliigos

	present	past	future
active participles	pliiganta	pliiginta	pliigonta
passive participles	pliigata	pliigita	pliigota

to introduce (a person to another person)	infinitive	imperative	conditional
	prezenti	prezentu	prezentus

indicative	present	past	future
	prezentas	prezentis	prezentos

	present	past	future
active participles	prezentanta	prezentinta	prezentonta
passive participles	prezentata	prezentita	prezentota

to invite	infinitive	imperative	conditional
	inviti	invitu	invitus

indicative	present	past	future
	invitas	invitis	invitos

	present	past	future
active participles	invitanta	invitinta	invitonta
passive participles	invitata	invitita	invitota

to kill	infinitive	imperative	conditional
	mor**tigi**	mor**tigu**	mor**tigus**

indicative	present	past	future
	mor**tigas**	mor**tigis**	mor**tigos**

	present	past	future
active participles	mor**tiganta**	mor**tiginta**	mor**tigonta**
passive participles	mor**tigata**	mor**tigita**	mor**tigota**

to kiss	infinitive	imperative	conditional
	kisi	**kisu**	**kisus**

indicative	present	past	future
	kisas	**kisis**	**kisos**

	present	past	future
active participles	**kisanta**	**kisinta**	**kisonta**
passive participles	**kisata**	**kisita**	**kisota**

to know	infinitive	imperative	conditional
	scii	**sciu**	**scius**

indicative	present	past	future
	scias	**sciis**	**scios**

	present	past	future
active participles	**scianta**	**sciinta**	**scionta**
passive participles	**sciata**	**sciita**	**sciota**

to laugh	infinitive	imperative	conditional
	ridi	**ri**du	**ri**dus

indicative	present	past	future
	ridas	**ri**dis	**ri**dos

	present	past	future
active participles	ri**dan**ta	ri**din**ta	ri**don**ta
passive participles	ri**da**ta	ri**di**ta	ri**do**ta

to learn	infinitive	imperative	conditional
	lerni	**ler**nu	**ler**nus

indicative	present	past	future
	lernas	**ler**nis	**ler**nos

	present	past	future
active participles	lern**an**ta	lern**in**ta	lern**on**ta
passive participles	lern**a**ta	lern**i**ta	lern**o**ta

to lie down, recline	infinitive	imperative	conditional
	ek**ku**ŝi	ek**ku**ŝu	ek**ku**ŝus

indicative	present	past	future
	ek**ku**ŝas	ek**ku**ŝis	ek**ku**ŝos

	present	past	future
active participles	ekku**ŝan**ta	ekku**ŝin**ta	ekku**ŝon**ta

to like	infinitive	imperative	conditional
	ŝati	ŝatu	ŝatus

indicative	present	past	future
	ŝatas	ŝatis	ŝatos

	present	past	future
active participles	ŝatanta	ŝatinta	ŝatonta
passive participles	ŝatata	ŝatita	ŝatota

to listen	infinitive	imperative	conditional
	aŭskulti	aŭskultu	aŭskultus

indicative	present	past	future
	aŭskultas	aŭskultis	aŭskultos

	present	past	future
active participles	aŭskultanta	aŭskultinta	aŭskultonta
passive participles	aŭskultata	aŭskultita	aŭskultota

to live, reside	infinitive	imperative	conditional
	loĝi	loĝu	loĝus

indicative	present	past	future
	loĝas	loĝis	loĝos

	present	past	future
active participles	loĝanta	loĝinta	loĝonta
passive participles	loĝata	loĝita	loĝota

to lose, to misplace	infinitive	imperative	conditional
	perdi	**per**du	**per**dus

indicative	present	past	future
	perdas	**per**dis	**per**dos

	present	past	future
active participles	per**dan**ta	per**din**ta	per**don**ta
passive participles	per**da**ta	per**di**ta	per**do**ta

to love	infinitive	imperative	conditional
	ami	**a**mu	**a**mus

indicative	present	past	future
	amas	**a**mis	**a**mos

	present	past	future
active participles	a**man**ta	a**min**ta	a**mon**ta
passive participles	a**ma**ta	a**mi**ta	a**mo**ta

to meet, encounter	infinitive	imperative	conditional
	ren**kon**ti	ren**kon**tu	ren**kon**tus

indicative	present	past	future
	ren**kon**tas	ren**kon**tis	ren**kon**tos

	present	past	future
active participles	renkon**tan**ta	renkon**tin**ta	renkon**ton**ta
passive participles	renkon**ta**ta	renkon**ti**ta	renkon**to**ta

to need	infinitive	imperative	conditional
	bezoni	bezonu	bezonus

indicative	present	past	future
	bezonas	bezonis	bezonos

	present	past	future
active participles	bezonanta	bezoninta	bezononta
passive participles	bezonata	bezonita	bezonota

to notice	infinitive	imperative	conditional
	rimarki	rimarku	rimarkus

indicative	present	past	future
	rimarkas	rimarkis	rimarkos

	present	past	future
active participles	rimarkanta	rimarkinta	rimarkonta
passive participles	rimarkata	rimarkita	rimarkota

to open something	infinitive	imperative	conditional
	malfermi	malfermu	malfermus

indicative	present	past	future
	malfermas	malfermis	malfermos

	present	past	future
active participles	malfermanta	malferminta	malfermonta
passive participles	malfermata	malfermita	malfermota

to play	infinitive	imperative	conditional
	ludi	**lu**du	**lu**dus

indicative	present	past	future
	ludas	**lu**dis	**lu**dos

	present	past	future
active participles	lu**dan**ta	lu**din**ta	lu**don**ta
passive participles	lu**da**ta	lu**di**ta	lu**do**ta

to put	infinitive	imperative	conditional
	meti	**me**tu	**me**tus

indicative	present	past	future
	metas	**me**tis	**me**tos

	present	past	future
active participles	me**tan**ta	me**tin**ta	me**ton**ta
passive participles	me**ta**ta	me**ti**ta	me**to**ta

to read	infinitive	imperative	conditional
	legi	**le**gu	**le**gus

indicative	present	past	future
	legas	**le**gis	**le**gos

	present	past	future
active participles	le**gan**ta	le**gin**ta	le**gon**ta
passive participles	le**ga**ta	le**gi**ta	le**go**ta

to receive	infinitive	imperative	conditional
	ricevi	ricevu	ricevus

indicative	present	past	future
	ricevas	ricevis	ricevos

	present	past	future
active participles	ricevanta	ricevinta	ricevonta
passive participles	ricevata	ricevita	ricevota

to remember	infinitive	imperative	conditional
	memori	memoru	memorus

indicative	present	past	future
	memoras	memoris	memoros

	present	past	future
active participles	memoranta	memorinta	memoronta
passive participles	memorata	memorita	memorota

to repeat	infinitive	imperative	conditional
	ripeti	ripetu	ripetus

indicative	present	past	future
	ripetas	ripetis	ripetos

	present	past	future
active participles	ripetanta	ripetinta	ripetonta
passive participles	ripetata	ripetita	ripetota

to return, go back	infinitive	imperative	conditional
	reveni	revenu	revenus

indicative	present	past	future
	revenas	revenis	revenos

	present	past	future
active participles	reve**nan**ta	reve**nin**ta	reve**non**ta

to run	infinitive	imperative	conditional
	kuri	**kur**u	**kur**us

indicative	present	past	future
	kuras	**kur**is	**kur**os

	present	past	future
active participles	kur**an**ta	kur**in**ta	kur**on**ta
passive participles	kur**a**ta	kur**i**ta	kur**o**ta

to say	infinitive	imperative	conditional
	diri	**dir**u	**dir**us

indicative	present	past	future
	diras	**dir**is	**dir**os

	present	past	future
active participles	dir**an**ta	dir**in**ta	dir**on**ta
passive participles	dir**a**ta	dir**i**ta	dir**o**ta

to scream	infinitive	imperative	conditional
	krii	**kri**u	**kri**us

indicative	present	past	future
	krias	**kri**is	**kri**os

	present	past	future
active participles	**kri**an**ta**	**kri**in**ta**	**kri**on**ta**
passive participles	**kri**a**ta**	**kri**i**ta**	**kri**o**ta**

to see	infinitive	imperative	conditional
	vidi	**vi**du	**vi**dus

indicative	present	past	future
	vidas	**vi**dis	**vi**dos

	present	past	future
active participles	**vi**dan**ta**	**vi**din**ta**	**vi**don**ta**
passive participles	**vi**da**ta**	**vi**di**ta**	**vi**do**ta**

to seem	infinitive	imperative	conditional
	ŝajni	**ŝaj**nu	**ŝaj**nus

indicative	present	past	future
	ŝajnas	**ŝaj**nis	**ŝaj**nos

	present	past	future
active participles	**ŝaj**nan**ta**	**ŝaj**nin**ta**	**ŝaj**non**ta**

to sell	infinitive	imperative	conditional
	vendi	**ven**du	**ven**dus

indicative	present	past	future
	vendas	**ven**dis	**ven**dos

	present	past	future
active participles	ven**dan**ta	ven**din**ta	ven**don**ta
passive participles	ven**da**ta	ven**di**ta	ven**do**ta

to send	infinitive	imperative	conditional
	sendi	**sen**du	**sen**dus

indicative	present	past	future
	sendas	**sen**dis	**sen**dos

	present	past	future
active participles	sen**dan**ta	sen**din**ta	sen**don**ta
passive participles	sen**da**ta	sen**di**ta	sen**do**ta

to show	infinitive	imperative	conditional
	montri	**mon**tru	**mon**trus

indicative	present	past	future
	montras	**mon**tris	**mon**tros

	present	past	future
active participles	mont**ran**ta	mont**rin**ta	mont**ron**ta
passive participles	mont**ra**ta	mont**ri**ta	mont**ro**ta

to sing	infinitive	imperative	conditional
	kanti	**kan**tu	**kan**tus

indicative	present	past	future
	kantas	**kan**tis	**kan**tos

	present	past	future
active participles	kan**tan**ta	kan**tin**ta	kan**ton**ta
passive participles	kan**tat**a	kan**tit**a	kan**tot**a

to sit, be sitting	infinitive	imperative	conditional
	sidi	**si**du	**si**dus

indicative	present	past	future
	sidas	**si**dis	**si**dos

	present	past	future
active participles	si**dan**ta	si**din**ta	si**don**ta

to sleep	infinitive	imperative	conditional
	dormi	**dor**mu	**dor**mus

indicative	present	past	future
	dormas	**dor**mis	**dor**mos

	present	past	future
active participles	dor**man**ta	dor**min**ta	dor**mon**ta

to smile	infinitive	imperative	conditional
	ri**de**ti	ri**de**tu	ri**de**tus

indicative	present	past	future
	ri**de**tas	ri**de**tis	ri**de**tos

	present	past	future
active participles	ride**tan**ta	ride**tin**ta	ride**ton**ta

to speak	infinitive	imperative	conditional
	pa**ro**li	pa**ro**lu	pa**ro**lus

indicative	present	past	future
	pa**ro**las	pa**ro**lis	pa**ro**los

	present	past	future
active participles	parol**an**ta	parol**in**ta	parol**on**ta
passive participles	paro**la**ta	paro**li**ta	paro**lo**ta

to stand, be standing	infinitive	imperative	conditional
	stari	**sta**ru	**sta**rus

indicative	present	past	future
	staras	**sta**ris	**sta**ros

	present	past	future
active participles	star**an**ta	star**in**ta	star**on**ta

to start something	infinitive	imperative	conditional
	komenci	komencu	komencus

indicative	present	past	future
	komencas	komencis	komencos

	present	past	future
active participles	komencanta	komencinta	komenconta
passive participles	komencata	komencita	komencota

to stay, remain	infinitive	imperative	conditional
	resti	restu	restus

indicative	present	past	future
	restas	restis	restos

	present	past	future
active participles	restanta	restinta	restonta

to take	infinitive	imperative	conditional
	preni	prenu	prenus

indicative	present	past	future
	prenas	prenis	prenos

	present	past	future
active participles	prenanta	preninta	prenonta
passive participles	prenata	prenita	prenota

to talk, chat	infinitive	imperative	conditional
	babili	babilu	babilus

indicative	present	past	future
	babilas	babilis	babilos

	present	past	future
active participles	babilanta	babilinta	babilonta
passive participles	babilata	babilita	babilota

to teach	infinitive	imperative	conditional
	instrui	instruu	instruus

indicative	present	past	future
	instruas	instruis	instruos

	present	past	future
active participles	instruanta	instruinta	instruonta
passive participles	instruata	instruita	instruota

to think	infinitive	imperative	conditional
	pensi	pensu	pensus

indicative	present	past	future
	pensas	pensis	pensos

	present	past	future
active participles	pensanta	pensinta	pensonta
passive participles	pensata	pensita	pensota

to touch	infinitive	imperative	conditional
	tuŝi	**tuŝu**	**tuŝus**

indicative	present	past	future
	tuŝas	**tuŝis**	**tuŝos**

	present	past	future
active participles	tuŝanta	tuŝinta	tuŝonta
passive participles	tuŝata	tuŝita	tuŝota

to travel	infinitive	imperative	conditional
	voĵaĝi	voĵaĝu	voĵaĝus

indicative	present	past	future
	voĵaĝas	voĵaĝis	voĵaĝos

	present	past	future
active participles	voĵaĝanta	voĵaĝinta	voĵaĝonta

to understand	infinitive	imperative	conditional
	komp**re**ni	komp**re**nu	komp**re**nus

indicative	present	past	future
	komp**re**nas	komp**re**nis	komp**re**nos

	present	past	future
active participles	kompre**nan**ta	kompre**nin**ta	kompre**non**ta
passive participles	kompre**na**ta	kompre**ni**ta	kompre**no**ta

to use	infinitive	imperative	conditional
	uzi	**u**zu	**u**zus

indicative	present	past	future
	uzas	**u**zis	**u**zos

	present	past	future
active participles	u**zan**ta	u**zin**ta	u**zon**ta
passive participles	u**za**ta	u**zi**ta	u**zo**ta

to wait	infinitive	imperative	conditional
	atendi	**aten**du	**aten**dus

indicative	present	past	future
	atendas	**aten**dis	**aten**dos

	present	past	future
active participles	atend**an**ta	atend**in**ta	atend**on**ta
passive participles	atend**a**ta	atend**i**ta	atend**o**ta

to walk	infinitive	imperative	conditional
	pie**di**ri	pie**di**ru	pie**di**rus

indicative	present	past	future
	pie**di**ras	pie**di**ris	pie**di**ros

	present	past	future
active participles	piedi**ran**ta	piedi**rin**ta	piedi**ron**ta
passive participles	piedi**ra**ta	piedi**ri**ta	piedi**ro**ta

to want	infinitive	imperative	conditional
	voli	**vo**lu	**vo**lus

indicative	present	past	future
	volas	**vo**lis	**vo**los

	present	past	future
active participles	vol**an**ta	vol**in**ta	vol**on**ta
passive participles	vol**a**ta	vol**i**ta	vol**o**ta

to watch	infinitive	imperative	conditional
	ri**gar**di	ri**gar**du	ri**gar**dus

indicative	present	past	future
	ri**gar**das	ri**gar**dis	ri**gar**dos

	present	past	future
active participles	rigard**an**ta	rigard**in**ta	rigard**on**ta
passive participles	rigard**a**ta	rigard**i**ta	rigard**o**ta

to win, to gain	infinitive	imperative	conditional
	gajni	**gaj**nu	**gaj**nus

indicative	present	past	future
	gajnas	**gaj**nis	**gaj**nos

	present	past	future
active participles	gaj**nan**ta	gaj**nin**ta	gaj**non**ta
passive participles	gaj**na**ta	gaj**ni**ta	gaj**no**ta

to work	infinitive	imperative	conditional
	labori	laboru	laborus

indicative	present	past	future
	laboras	laboris	laboros

	present	past	future
active participles	laboranta	laborinta	laboronta

to write	infinitive	imperative	conditional
	skribi	skribu	skribus

indicative	present	past	future
	skribas	skribis	skribos

	present	past	future
active participles	skribanta	skribinta	skribonta
passive participles	skribata	skribita	skribota

13847677R00035

Printed in Poland
by Amazon Fulfillment
Poland Sp. z o.o., Wrocław